Marbles, marbles, looking fine.
Which line shows us 1 plus 9?

For my friend Sister Cathy Molloy,
teacher and on-site project coordinator
of the OK Clean Water Project
in Kumbo, Cameroon
—J. M.

For my nephews
Noah and Owen
—C. P.

Library of Congress Cataloging-in-Publication Data
Marzollo, Jean.
Help me learn addition / by Jean Marzollo ; photographs by Chad Phillips. — 1st American ed.
p. cm.
ISBN 978-0-8234-2398-9 (hardcover)
1. Addition—Juvenile literature.
I. Phillips, Chad, ill. II. Title.
QA115.M33 2012
513.2'11—dc23
2011024037

Help Me Learn Addition

by **Jean Marzollo**

photographs by

Chad Phillips

Holiday House / New York

How many puppets? Look alive!
We count 1, 2, 3, 4, _____ (5).
The number 5 is the last we say.
So that's the answer. Hip hooray!

1, 2, 3, 4, 5. Can't wait!

Count on: 6, 7, _____ (8).

The number 8 is the last we say.

So that's the answer. Hip hooray!

We like to count,
but we are glad
that now we're learning
how to add.

What is the answer
when we add zero?
It's what we had.
Is that clear-o?

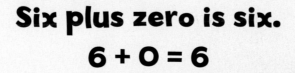

Six plus zero is six.
6 + 0 = 6

What is the answer
when we add one?
We count one more.
That's it! We're done.

Six plus one is seven.
6 + 1 = 7

Here comes the math train
straight from Penn!
7 plus 3
equals 10.

7 + 3 = 10

The math train is
coming back again!
3 + 7
also equals 10.

3 + 7 = 10

Here's a question
for you and me.
Does 3 plus 7
equal 7 plus 3?

It took a long time
to count our pigs today.
So we have a question.
Is there a faster way?

1   2   3   4   5   6   7   8   9   10

Yes!
Put 5 pigs in a basket.
Put 5 pigs in a pen.
Add 5 and 5,
and we get _____ (10).

We can also skip count
like this: 5, _____ (10).

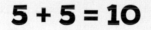

5 + 5 = 10

5
+5
———
10

We have 8 little chicks,
add 1 more, and then ...
we add 1 more.
Now we have _____ (10).

8 + 1 + 1 = 10

Our chicks paired off,
which helps us when
we skip count
2, 4, 6, 8, _____ (10).

2 + 2 + 2 + 2 + 2 = 10

Now let's study 10 again.

0 + 10

1 + 9

2 + 8

3 + 7

4 + 6

5 + 5

6 + 4

7 + 3

8 + 2

9 + 1

10 + 0

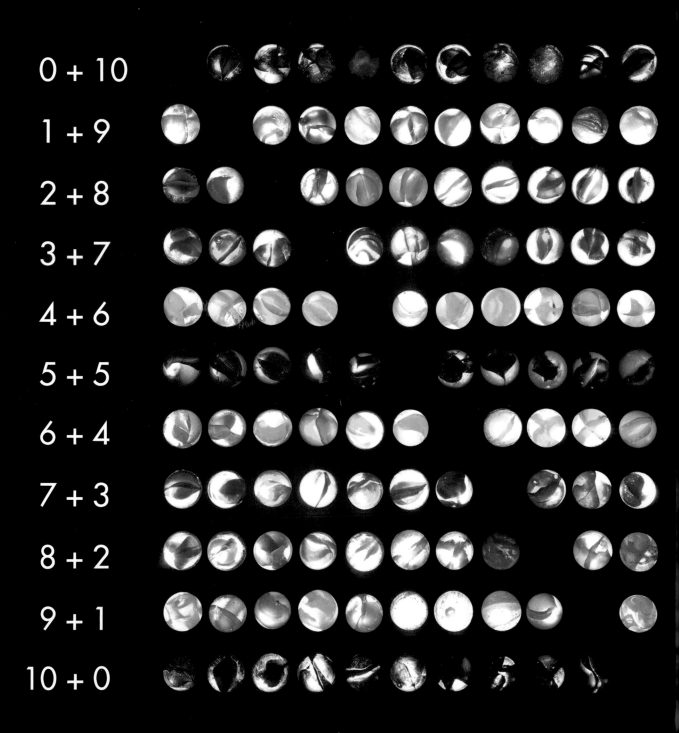

Can you say these ways to get to 10?

10 + 0

9 + 1

8 + 2

7 + 3

6 + 4

5 + 5

4 + 6

3 + 7

2 + 8

1 + 9

0 + 10

Here's a monster challenge
for us mathematicians today.
Can we add up to 10
in a 3-part way?

We could make a group of 5,
add a group of 1,
then add a group of 4.
That's it. We're done!

$$
\begin{array}{r}
5 \\
1 \\
+\ 4 \\
\hline
10
\end{array}
$$

Can we add up to 10
in a 4-part way?

2 + 3 + 3 + 2 = 10

And then and then
and then and then . . . .
What other ways
can we add up
to 10?

How many little animals?
We count them and we know
the last number is the answer;
and that is simply so.

1, 2, 3, 4, 5, 6, 7, 8, 9, 10, 11

Now it is Addition Time!
Here's a number sentence rhyme.

3 + 2 = 5

5 + 2 = 7

7 + 3 = 10

10 + 1 = 11

How many dogs
have we seen?
10 plus 4.
That makes _____ (14).

10 + 4 = 14

How many now
have we seen?
10 plus 1
plus 3 _____ (14).

10
1
+ 3
———
14

Spaceship babies
want to know more.
Can we tell them
what tally marks are for?

Tally marks help
us count today.
Here's a math sentence
the tally mark way.

$$\text{卌} + \text{|||} + \text{|} = 9$$

More space babies.
Now we have plenty!
5, 10, 15, _____ (20).

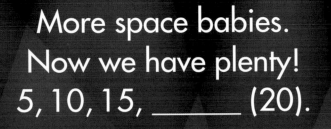

$$||||| + ||||| + ||||| + ||||| = \textbf{20}$$

Are you ready
for some action?
Here's a preview
of subtraction.

8 strawberries!
That's great!

But someone greedy
ate all 8.

$8 - 8 = 0$

That story was sad.
Let's subtract again
in a new berry story.
Let's start with 10.

An owl with 10 berries she wanted to share

gave 5 to a friend because that was fair.

10 − 5 = 5 That's subtraction!

Dear Parents and Teachers,

The purpose of this book is to help young children enjoy the experience of learning addition so that they will be ready to succeed in kindergarten today.

Based on the Common Core State Standards, kindergarten children, by the end of the school year, are expected to work with numbers from 0–20. They learn how to make groups of objects to add together and how to skip count groups of objects. They learn that the numbers between 11 and 19 are sums of a group of 10 and some 1s. They also learn to create number sentences such as 10 + 2 = 12.

You can help your child think about addition at an early age. Just as you would naturally count with a toddler, you also can hold up two cars and playfully say, "One car plus one car makes two cars!" Toddlers, preschoolers, and kindergartners enjoy the pictures and rhymes in this book. They like to open their hands and say, "5, 10!" As they grow, they will understand more about addition.

If you pause at the end of each verse, your child may finish it for you. The rhyme is a clue to the answer. Older children may memorize the rhymes and like to read or pretend to read them to you.

As you playfully add familiar objects, feel proud that you are starting your child down the path to addition!

Happy adding,
Jean Marzollo

Grateful Thanks

We would like to thank Grace Wilkie, past president, Association of Mathematics Teachers of New York State and member of the New York State Mathematics Hall of Fame. Grace helped us understand the Common Core State Standards. As Grace explained, "Seeing a child go from counting to addition is the first of many critical mathematical steps. Having a child hold up both of their hands, see ten digits, and then associate them with the number ten is exciting. Learning and appreciating mathematics at a young age sets a child's foundation for years."

To learn more about these standards, please go to: www.corestandards.org.

We thank Grace Maccarone, our editor, and Claire Counihan, our art director, at Holiday House for continuing the HELP ME LEARN series that began with *Help Me Learn Numbers 0–20*.

We'd like to thank Maggie Davis and Betsy Rasa at Haldane Elementary School in Cold Spring, New York, for their helpful advice.

We thank Bob and Barbara Wade of Once Upon A Time Antiques in Cold Spring, New York. Their fascinating toy store is where we found the ducks, trains, pigs, chicks, marbles, dogs, and owls. We thank Archie McPhee & Co. for giving us permission to use the monster finger puppets (adding to ten picture) and Virginia Bjorgum of Nature's Accents for giving permission to use the Brushkins. We thank Sanyork, Inc. for permission to use the Peruvian hand-knit finger puppets and U.S. Toy Co. for permission to use the chunky monster finger puppets (tally marks picture).

Jean Marzollo and Chad Phillip

Marbles, marbles, we have plenty.

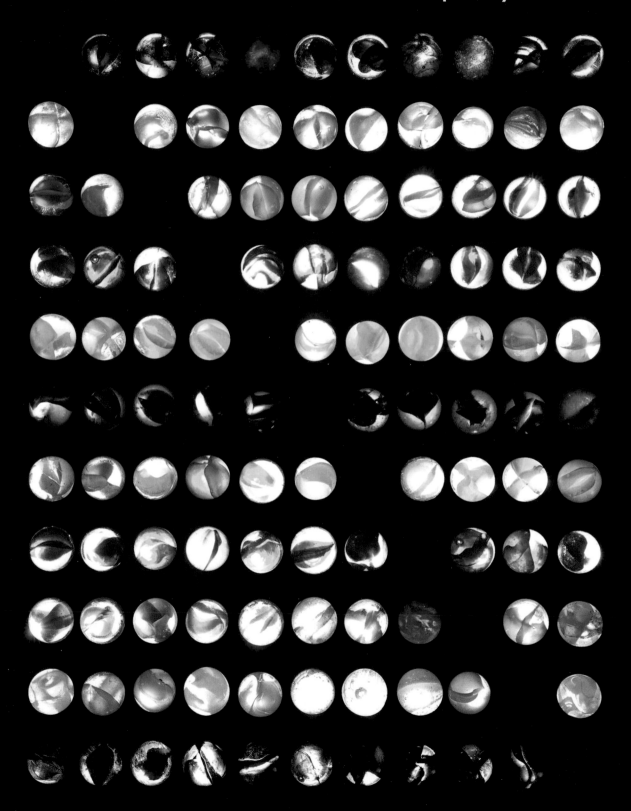